Danny Johnson

IF I TELL YOU A HEN DIPS SNUFF...

By Bob Bowman

IF I TELL YOU A HEN DIPS SNUFF...

By Bob Bowman

Lufkin Printing Company
Post Office Box 589
Lufkin, Texas 75901

Other books by Bob Bowman

This Was East Texas
The Towns We Left Behind
They Left No Monuments
Land of the Little Angel (Editor)
The Best of East Texas

To a multitude of friends
who encouraged and contributed
to this effort.

FOREWORD

If there's anything that sets a good ol' boy from Texas apart from the rest of the world, it's the way he talks.

Sandwiched between the cowboy culture of the Southwest and the down-home heritage of the Old South, Texans over the years have developed a distinctive way of expressing themselves—a linguistic potpourri of farm-boy homilies, ranch-hand proverbs, and log-cutter sayings. It's a language that draws heavily on rural experiences—hunting, fishing, and man's tenacious struggle with the soil and weather—and relates those experiences to contemporary life.

"The squeaking wheel always get the grease" may not mean much to a Dallas or Houston resident who has lived most of his life in metropolitan or surburban environs, but an East Texan readily understands that it means the worse a problem gets, the more attention it deserves.

Many of the expressions found here are old, dating back to the Depression era when row-crop farming was a way of life. Many are the creation of rural people who related the vagaries of human nature with problems they faced with mules, dogs and troublesome women.

Others are comparatively new, the product of fertile imaginations or unique events. To illustrate, Bob Murphey, every East Texan's favorite humorist, tells the story about the Dallas man who came down to the piney woods to visit his elderly aunt and uncle.

When nightfall arrived, the couple prepared for bed, and the nephew overheard this conversation.

"Maw, did you put out the cat?"

"Yes."

"Did you wind the clock?"

"Yes."

"Did you turn the rooster?"

"Yes."

The nephew wondered about the last expression—one he had never heard—and at breakfast the next morning, he asked what it meant.

"Well," said his uncle, " a few months ago, your aunt found this scrawny little chick abandoned out in the yard by the ol' mother hen. She took him in the house, took care of him, and he growed up to be a pretty big ol' rooster."

"But now we can't get him out of the house. Every time we throw him out, he somehow finds his way back inside. And every night, he roosts there in the kitchen on the edge of the flour barrel."

"And before we go to bed, we want to make dang sure the rooster is turned the right way."

While the language of the good ol' boy still flourishes today in Texas, the sad truth is that its days are likely numbered. The merging of Texas' divergent cultures, modern education and communication techniques, and the passing of a rural-oriented generation are taking their toll.

Hopefully, this work will play some small part in helping to preserve Texas' unique expressions for future generations.

But there's still work to be done. While we've tried to include between 700 and 800 of the most significant idioms, there are hundreds more which deserve equal attention.

As you examine the expressions found here, you may find yourself disagreeing with the author on the meaning we've attached to them. That's to be expected; many of the expressions have more than one meaning, depending on how it is used and who is doing the speaking.

Finally, we would be negligent if we failed to thank the hundreds of individuals who over the years have shared with us their expressions and encouraged us to produce this collection.

A special word of appreciation is due three dear friends—Ottis Lock, Ben Ramsey and Ed Clark—for permitting us to eavesdrop on their enlivened conversations over the last decade or so. The well-peppered debates and bantor of these three grand old men of Texas politics did more than anything else to inspire this book.

Bob Bowman
Lufkin, Texas

CONTENTS

CHAPTER 1

If I tell you a hen dips snuff, you can look under her wing.

You can rest assured I'm telling you the truth.

Friendly as a bootlegger

Pretends to be a friend, but has a selfish interest in the relationship.

I've been listening to the grapevine telegraph.

I've been hearing rumors.

She peeled my eye and bent my ear.

She likes to gossip.

Dressed up like a dirt road dude.

A country dandy who puts on his best clothes and goes into town every Saturday.

You could ride to town on that blade without a blanket.

A dull knife.

Just a lil' ol' bill.

A Texas legislator's label for legislation "that won't bother anybody."

He seldom comes out of the same hole.

Like a burrowing animal, he is elusive and frequently changes directions.

That ol' gal is common as hog tracks.

Unattractive.

He could bite through a side of bacon without greasing a gum.

He has a big mouth.

Hair in the butter.

A sensitive situation.

He saucers and blows his coffee.

A country boy or farmer who cools his coffee by pouring it into a saucer and blowing on it.

He must've been hit with a wet cob when he was young.

He's not too bright.

Church ain't out 'till the fat lady sings.

Don't act prematurely; wait until you get all the facts.

Crooked as a barrel of snakes.

Dishonest.

There's something seldom about that ol' boy.

He's a little strange.

He sure lets a lot fall through the cracks.

Careless; rarely attentive to details.

I've got to kill a chicken and churn.

It's time to go home; I've got housework to do.

I'll do it if it hairlips every mule in Texas.

An expression of determination.

He came at me from six sides.

1. He was angry. 2. He whipped me in a fight.

Tail deep to a tall Indian.

Short.

He don't tote level.

Unreliable.

Don't make love by the garden gate. Love is blind but the neighbors ain't.

Be discreet in courting.

I had it in me as big as a horse.

I was sure I could do it.

Hen apples.

Eggs.

Are you gonna fish or cut bait?

Stop fooling around and finish what you started.

He'd fight a rattlesnake and give it two bites to start.

Fearless.

He goes all around ol' Jake's barn.

Long-winded; takes a long time to make a point.

He came down here big-eyeing around.

Acting important, pompus.

He flew off the handle.

He lost his temper.

Tush hog.

A community leader, an important person.

I feel like a whupped dog.

Tired, weary.

Suit-case company.

Overnight visitors, usually relatives.

ow off on my new horse.

ng.

ead.

liced bread.

ke down and gave in.

carrying on.

all-screwed-up cold.

ther.

bell you hear ain't the dinner

act to circumstances too quickly.

was like a one-eyed dog in a
kehouse.

was having a good time. 2. Too much of a good thing.

died of hisself.

ural death.

ll, dog bite my buttons!

expression of exclamation.

andy as the top rail on the fence.

eful.

You shouldn't go talking about ropes in the house of a hanged man.

Be discreet in what you say.

I hear you clucking, but I can't find your nest.

I don't understand what you're saying.

He did it quicker'n a minnow can swim a dipper.

Acted speedily.

Land-poor.

He doesn't have much cash, but lots of land.

His hogs are so poor it takes six of them to make a shadow.

Poverty stricken.

I'm hunkered down.

Prepared.

He's all horns and rattles.

Displaying a temper.

High as a cat's back.

Costly.

Big as all-Dallas./Bigger'n Dallas.

Expansive, large.

Scarce as hen's teeth and frog fangs.

A rare occurance.

If it ain't broke, don't fix it.

Don't get involved unless you have to.

Busier than a one-legged man in a butt-kicking contest.

A busy man.

He was just about three sheets in the wind.

Drunk.

He looks like death warmed over.

In poor health.

Floored and frenzied.

Drunk.

He was grinning like a mule eating briars.

Caught in an embarassing situation.

He sure enough ripped his britches.

Made a mistake.

He took his hat in his hand.

He humbled himself.

Don't go t[...] its liable t[...]

Don't accuse someb[...] facts.

This log is s[...] still.

A situation difficult to re[...]

Even a blind [...] every once in a[...]

Everybody gets lucky occasi[...]

That ol' woman [...] jebes.

She's strange.

I just as soon sack[...]

This is a difficult task and I hate to [...]

If you play with fir[...] you'll wet the bed 'fo[...]

A mother's warning to children playing [...]

They're steeple people[...]

A description of city church members, [...] steeples. Used by rural residents, whose ch[...]

That ol' woman has granr[...] kids in the county.

She's like a grandmother to a lot of people: be[...]

Don't thr[...]

Don't be insulti[...]

Light br[...]

Store-bought s[...]

He brok[...]

Acquiesced.

She's [...]

Excitable.

It was[...]

Frigid wea[...]

Every[...] bell.

Don't rea[...]

He [...] smo[...]

1. He [...]

He [...]

A na[...]

W[...]

An [...]

H[...]

Us[...]

Deaf in one ear and can't hear out of the other.

Hard of hearing.

He can't see through a bob-wire fence.

Lacks understanding.

Fine as frog's hair.

I'm pleased.

I'm so tired I could sleep on a bob-wire fence.

Weary.

He's itching for a licking./He's aching for a breaking./He's cruisin' for a bruisin'.

1. He made me mad. 2. He's in trouble.

That was hard-down good.

Excellent.

I've got a gravy train with biscuit wheels.

Easy living.

His tongue was hanging out a foot and forty inches.

He was hot and tired.

Gravel in his gizzard.

A rugged individual.

Chugged full.

Filled to capacity.

This is a mare's nest.

Confusing.

That was a right smart meal./That was the best meal I ever lapped a lip over.

An excellent meal.

She has her cap set for him.

She intends to marry him.

Useless as teats on a boar hog.

Of no value.

I'm tired of cleaning up your messes.

I'm weary of correcting your mistakes.

Now, ain't that the berries?

Isn't that something?

The preacher has started talking to the pulpit committee.

The minister is bored with his congregation, and plans to join another church.

His didy pin must be sticking him.
Childish.

His eyes bugged out so far you could've roped them.
He was amazed.

God looks after drunks, fools and babies.
Somehow, they all seem to survive the worst.

Green as a gourd.
Naive.

It ain't worth a whet or a whittle.
Of little value.

He's cooking up syrup.
Performing a productive effort.

Tough as rawhide.
Durable.

I'm too pooped to pop.
Weary.

Shut my mouth!
I'm speechless.

That would gag a maggot.
Distasteful.

I've been ran down, run over and wrung out.

It's been a hard day.

He's hell on leather./He's hell on wheels.

1. An untiring worker. 2. A tempermental person.

The latchstring is out.

You're welcome.

CHAPTER 2

He's sorry as homemade soap.

Irresponsible.

Nervous as a whore in a church house.

Jumpy.

He's like trying to hem up hot syrup with half a biscuit.

1. Hard to pin down on a decision. 2. Disorganized.

It won't kill him, but it'll worm him good.

Usually a reference to moonshine liquor.

Straighter'n a sapling.

Dependable, honest.

She tamed that ol' boy at an all-civilized rate.

1. She calmed down an angry man. 2. She married an angry man and made him hen-pecked.

That rain was regular gully-washer and fence-lifter (or a gully-washer and root-searcher)./It's raining bull frogs and heifer yearlings.

That was some rain.

The squeaking wheel always get the grease.

The worse a problem becomes, the more attention it needs.

It rained just enough to run.

A light shower.

He plows a deep row.

A deep thinker.

Pick-'em-up truck.

Pickup truck.

He tried to trade me a turnip for a Tennessee walking horse.

It was a poor trade.

Tol'able.

Doing well.

The Lord poured in his brains with a thimble, and somebody shook His hand.

He isn't very smart.

She couldn't carry a tune in a sack.

Doesn't sing well.

I'll do it by the second Tuesday of next week.

I'll get around to it when I can.

She chased me all over hell and half of Texas.

A large area.

It's time to taw down.

I'm ready to discuss a trade.

He's toted a lot of wood and water for them.

He has strong attachments with someone.

The morning rain is like an old woman's dance. It's soon over.

A short rainfall.

It's like looking for a whisper in a twister.

Impossible.

This water is so muddy that the fish have to swim backwards to keep the mud out of their eyes.

Muddy river or creek.

I hope you'll act white about this.

Do the right thing.

I've seen wilder heifers than you milked in a gourd.

You say that you're tough, but I don't believe you.

You can't tell how deep the well is by measuring the length of the pump handle.

Looks can be deceiving.

He's wetting on my leg, but it feels warm.

He's flattering me, but I like it.

I think that ol' gal swallowed a watermelon seed.

A pregnant woman.

It's as useless as a hip pocket on a hog.

Worthless.

She's ready to wade deep water.

A woman in a short skirt.

He carries around a window sash wrapped in a Baptist Standard.

He speaks softly, but acts decisively.

If you've got an ax to grind, you ain't gonna chop much wood.

Don't let your personal prejudices get involved in your effort to do a good job.

He's in his best bib and tucker.

An elegant dresser.

He's tight as the bark on a hickory tree.

Stingy.

My eyes were bigger'n my belly.

I ate too much.

Mexican strawberries.

Beans.

Like a bowlegged man trying to hem up a hog in a ditch.

Not very productive.

She don't know split beans from coffee.

Doltish.

He boogied off downtown.

Wandered off.

I don't think his dipping took.

A Baptist backslider.

He took off like a Martin to his gourd.

He went straight to his destination.

Bell cow.

A community leader, one respected by everyone.

More cotton will grow in a crooked row than a straight one.

The best things aren't always easily accessible.

Hotter'n a pot of collards.

Angry.

It's time to shell down the corn and cut the cob.

Let's get down to business.

He straightened out that curve.

He had an automobile accident.

Don't that just beat a hen a-scratching?/Don't that just beat a hen a-loping?

I'm impressed.

He came up short on the gettin' end./He's not playing with a full deck./He didn't get a full dose.

Simple-minded.

18

An accident looking for a place to happen.

A poor driver.

Gotch-eyed.

Cross-eyed.

He growed up on collards.

Someone who has lived most of his live in a rural area.

We're last cousins.

Distant kinship.

He's so crooked he can sleep in the shade of a post hole auger.

Deceitful.

I've seen cows hurt worse than this and get well.

A reference to a poorly-cooked or rare steak.

He's so crooked he has to screw on his socks.

A devious individual.

I can't come it.

1. I don't like it. 2. I can't do what you've asked.

That ol' dog won't hunt no more.

That might have worked before, but not this time.

Cold coon and collards.

A pot luck supper.

I've got a crow to pick with you./I've got a row to hoe with you.

I need to discuss something serious with you.

He's up Salt Creek./He's in a regular jack-pot./He's done messed up.

In big trouble.

That ol' woman has a face so long she can eat oats out of a churn.

A sour disposition.

Meaner'n a yaller yard dog.

Easy to anger.

Let's get past the house before the dogs start barking.

Let's get this business resolved before someone starts complaining.

He's back from Boozer City.

Drunk. Boozer City is a reference to Boosier City, La., known for its taverns and bars.

Shoot me a star, Lord.

An expression used by a Negro after experiencing a religious conversion, asking God to give him a sign—usually a shooting star in the night sky—that his conversion was genuine.

You shouldn't go talking about ropes in the house of a hanged man.

Be discreet in what you say.

I hear you clucking, but I can't find your nest.

I don't understand what you're saying.

He did it quicker'n a minnow can swim a dipper.

Acted speedily.

Land-poor.

He doesn't have much cash, but lots of land.

His hogs are so poor it takes six of them to make a shadow.

Poverty stricken.

I'm hunkered down.

Prepared.

He's all horns and rattles.

Displaying a temper.

High as a cat's back.

Costly.

Big as all-Dallas./Bigger'n Dallas.

Expansive, large.

Scarce as hen's teeth and frog fangs.

A rare occurance.

If it ain't broke, don't fix it.

Don't get involved unless you have to.

Busier than a one-legged man in a butt-kicking contest.

A busy man.

He was just about three sheets in the wind.

Drunk.

He looks like death warmed over.

In poor health.

Floored and frenzied.

Drunk.

He was grinning like a mule eating briars.

Caught in an embarassing situation.

He sure enough ripped his britches.

Made a mistake.

He took his hat in his hand.

He humbled himself.

Don't throw off on my new horse.

Don't be insulting.

Light bread.

Store-bought sliced bread.

He broke down and gave in.

Acquiesced.

She's carrying on.

Excitable.

It was all-screwed-up cold.

Frigid weather.

Every bell you hear ain't the dinner bell.

Don't react to circumstances too quickly.

He was like a one-eyed dog in a smokehouse.

1. He was having a good time. 2. Too much of a good thing.

He died of hisself.

A natural death.

Well, dog bite my buttons!

An expression of exclamation.

Handy as the top rail on the fence.

Useful.

Don't go throwing manure uphill, or its liable to roll back in your face.

Don't accuse somebody of something when you aren't sure of the facts.

This log is so crooked it won't lay still.

A situation difficult to resolve.

Even a blind hog finds an acorn every once in a while.

Everybody gets lucky occasionally.

That ol' woman gives me the hebe-jebes.

She's strange.

I just as soon sack up bobcats.

This is a difficult task and I hate to undertake it.

If you play with fire at sundown, you'll wet the bed 'fore sunup.

A mother's warning to children playing with fire.

They're steeple people.

A description of city church members, whose churches had steeples. Used by rural residents, whose churches were plain.

That ol' woman has grannied half the kids in the county.

She's like a grandmother to a lot of people: beloved.

Let's likker one more round.

Let's have another drink.

That ol' dog won't bite biscuits.

Gentle, not too aggressive.

I don't care if syrup goes to a dollar a sop.

1. I'm not bothered by the cost. 2. I intend to finish the job.

He'll trail a dog anywhere he can carry him.

He'll go hunting anywhere, anytime.

The skunk can't tell the buzzard he stinks.

A person guilty of a fault shouldn't accuse another of the same.

He's a hard dog to keep under the wagon.

Difficult to keep out of trouble.

Every sausage knows if it's made out of hog or dog.

Every individual knows his own worth.

You're leading your ducks to the wrong pond./You're barking up the wrong tree.

You're mistaken.

He ran out like a scalded dog.

Frightened.

I didn't go to do it.

I'm sorry; I didn't mean it.

Who stuck the burr under your saddle?

Who made you mad?

I feel like I've been pulling a dull saw all day long.

Fatigued.

He shot his best hunting dog.

He made a mistake which cost him dearly.

She can't drive nails in the snow.

Inept.

All painted up like a new honky-tonk.

A woman out for a good time.

Sure enough? How come?

Is that right?

All he owns is the shirt on his back, and the buttons are on account.

Impoverished.

The sun don't shine on the same ol' dog's tail all the time.

Circumstances change eventually.

She sews with a hot needle and burnt thread.

A poor seamstress.

All out of snuff.

Weary.

Modest dogs don't get much meat.

Those who are reluctant to act may not achieve much.

Spoutin' steam at every joint.

Infuriated.

Don't that just rot your socks?

Isn't that surprising?

Lower than a snake's hips.

Furtive in nature.

Nobody ever drownded in a sweat.

Hard work never hurt anyone.

Loop-legged.

Drunk.

He jobbed him.

He poked or stabbed someone.

He's not as big as a bar of soap after a day's washing.

Small in stature.

Fire-hunters.

Illegal deer hunters who spot deer at night by directing a beam of light into their eyes.

I didn't know it was hungry 'till it swallowed me up and spit me out.

I failed to recognize the danger of the situation.

She was madder'n a wet hen.

Angry.

CHAPTER 3

Ugly as homemade sin./Ugly as a mud fence./Homely enough to sour milk.

Uncomely.

It's time to put the chairs in the wagon.

Time to leave or go home.

She's a right nice heifer.

An attractive woman.

Sto'wood.

Wood for the stove.

It's coming up a cloud.

The weather is worsening.

He ain't worth the powder and lead it would take to blow him up.

Of little value.

It clouded up and rained knuckles.

A rain storm.

Now, it takes a big woman to weigh a ton.

Are you positive about your statement?

Green as a cut-seed watermelon.

Gullible.

That guinea's not worth the salt.

Second rate.

He's gone back on his raisin'.

He forgot what his parents taught him.

It's a long road that don't turn.

1. Things will eventually change. 2. Things will get better.

Quiet as a sick sow in a snowstorm.

Doesn't make much noise.

He's liable to break his arm pattin' hisself on the back.

A prideful man.

She gave it a lick and a promise.

She did the job only half-well.

It's too wet to plow.

This isn't the right time.

A plowman on his knees is higher than a rich man on his legs.

A poor, God-fearing man is just as important as a wealthy man.

Come visit, and we'll put the kids down a Baptist pallet.

We'll let the children sleep on blankets and the floor.

There ain't no disgrace in being poor, but it sure is downright inconvenient.

It would be nice to have a little more money.

Stump water.

Foul-tasting.

Poor as a lizard-eating cat.

Poverty-stricken.

You can never get all the 'possums (or 'coons) up the same tree.

It's hard to do everything at once.

There was never a persimmon 'cept there was a 'possum to eat it.

For every action, there has to be a reaction.

They'll stay until the last peas are out of the pot.

Visitors who don't leave until all of the food has been eaten.

He's plowing new ground.

Starting something new.

He doesn't have a pot to wet in or a window to throw it out of.

Poor.

Motherless peas.

Peas cooked without pork.

His promises are like pie crusts.

You can't depend on what he tells you.

He looks peak'd.

Pale, sickly-looking.

Porch sitters.

Loafers, usually found on the porch of a country store.

He's running in my ruts.

He's following me around.

The faster I go, the behinder I get.

The harder I work, the less I achieve.

He just rode in on a load of water-melons.

He isn't too sophisticated.

It looks like it's fairing off.

The weather is improving.

We'uns been, you'uns come.

It's your turn to visit at our house.

I don't understand a lick of what he said.

It doesn't make sense.

He's making three tracks in the dirt.

He's so tired he's dragging.

She stomped all over my toes.

She rebuked me.

Every tub has to stand on its own bottom.

Each person is responsible for his actions.

Full as a tick.

Overindulged.

He's thin as a rail.

Scrawny, frail-looking.

Snake-bit.

Unlucky.

It's hard to make the tongue and the buckle meet.

1. Impossible to achieve. 2. The size of your girth depends on how much you eat.

She took a liking to him./She's taken to him.

Attracted to a man.

Sharp as a steel trap and bright as a pewter button.

Quick-witted, clever.

It tastes so good it would make a boy slap his granny.

A culinary delight.

Distant stovewood is the best stovewood.

The best things in life are worth looking for.

Watch out or you'll plow up snakes.

Be careful what you say or you'll create a problem.

I got the short end of this stick.

Short-changed; treated unfairly.

He'll do to run the river with.

He's the kind of companion you'd like to have along when you run your troutlines in the river. Cowboys also used the expression for someone who helped herd cattle across a river.

He's soap-tracked and spinning his wheels.

1. He's talking but not making much sense. 2. He is making an effort to do the job, but isn't getting anywhere.

Tacky as all get out.
Slovenly in appearance.

Slow as syrup in February.
Sluggish in nature.

Slick as a peeled cucumber.
Canny, quick-witted.

That ol' man sits in the shade of the tree to save the shade of the porch.
Tight-fisted.

He'll steal money off a dead man's eyes.
Dishonest.

He'd kill a flea for the hide and tallow.
Stingy.

Smart as a two-bit whip.
Intelligent, alert.

You can't beat that with a hickory stick.
1. I approve. 2. A good arrangement.

He slobbered in his messkit.
Misfortune which cost him personally.

Too sorry to hit a lick at a snake.

Too lazy to look after his own welfare.

He must've been dropped off St. Peter's coattails.

A pious individual.

They've gone to the skillet.

They journeyed to the Texas Panhandle.

Man's the only animal that can be skinned more than once.

Man is gullible.

Spitting in the wind.

An unproductive effort.

I don't know him from the side of shoe leather.

He's not a friend of mine.

Tote your own skillet.

Look after your own interests.

They were shirt-sleeves to shirt-sleeves in three generations.

Most of the men in our family have been working men.

It was longer'n a month of Sundays.

A prolonged period of time.

He don't know scat from scout.

Uninformed.

It's like bailing out the boat with a teaspoon.

It isn't worth the effort.

Thunderbucket.

A slop jar.

Get down (or come in) and cool the seat of your saddle.

Come in and visit for a while.

He's wetter'n a drownded rat.

Soaked.

It's like trying to get the river to run over the bridge.

Impossible to do.

He jumped at the first rattle out of the box.

He moved quickly.

Rozzum.

Pine resin.

Hotter'n a depot stove.

Aggravated.

Nervous as a cat in a room full of rockers.

Jumpy.

Now, if that don't take the rag off the bush.

That's the ultimate.

He ought to be playing with a string of spools.

He's not very mature.

He has lots of speed but no control.

He has the ability, but poor judgment.

The rich get richer and the poor get children.

It's hard for a poor man to get ahead.

CHAPTER 4

Bad breath is better'n none at all.

Despite our faults, it's good to be alive.

That ol' buck had a set of horns like a rockin' chair.

A deer with an impressive rack.

An empty bucket makes the most racket.

A shallow or superficial person usually talks a lot, but says nothing of importance.

Busy as a stump-tailed cow in summer time.

Overworked.

Some folks are all right until they get two pair of britches.

Prosperity often affects people adversely.

He has his tail in a crack.

He's in trouble; he's angry.

Company, like new bread, goes stale after three days.

Visitors become bothersome if they stay too long.

He's been stomping around in cow-piles most of his life.

1. A country boy. 2. His life has been marked by misfortune.

She could make a good meal out of a bone's smell.

A good cook.

Everybody who says good night ain't going home.

Courting usually begins after a party.

He cusses like chickens coming to roost.

A profane man.

If you fixed up a pot of coffee in hell, he'd go after it.

An avid coffee drinker.

All he gave me was an inch of cord-wood and an ounce of cornshucks.

He failed to finish the job I gave him.

They split the blanket.

Divorce; separation.

That coffee is too thick to drink and too thin to plow.

Black, strong coffee.

You might as well die with the chills as the fever.

A man trapped between two dilemmas; caught between a rock and a hard place.

He ain't got no more chance than a kerosene cat in hell.

A hopeless situation.

Colder'n an outhouse seat on a December morning.

It's cold.

Looked like something the cat drug up.

Sloppy, slovenly.

Rougher'n a cob and twice as long.

He's a rugged individual.

It was measured with a 'coon skin with the tail throwed in.

The measurement wasn't fair; it was more than what it should have been.

He's happy as if he had good sense.

Jovial; pleased with the results.

I had a piece of pie the size of a baby's high chair.

I ate too much.

Tell them how the cow ate the cabbage.

Tell the truth.

You can load gold on a mule, but he's still a mule.

You can't change a man's basic nature.

I'll dance with them what brung me.

I'll stick with my friends.

Too much of a good thing is dog's bait.

Even the best things become tedious after a while.

There's more than one way to break a hound from sucking eggs.

This job can be done several ways.

He's so drunk he couldn't hit the ground with his hat after three throws.

Inebriated.

I've had a bait of that!

I've had enough.

Doesn't have the sense to pull in his head when he shuts the window.

Simple-minded.

Lord, you're a sight for sore eyes.

It's good to see you.

It's not what you want that makes you fat, but what you get.

Willpower is the only way you can control your weight.

His eyes were stickin' out like the cow catcher on a switch engine.

He looked on in amazement.

Having as much fun as a tomcat in a fish store.

Enjoyable.

A fool talks with his ears stuffed up.

A vain person doesn't pay much attention to what others are saying.

She's flirtin' like a Spanish filly.

Making passes at a man.

Booze blind.

Drunk.

Drunker'n a fiddler's bitch.

Soused.

She has on a brand splinterfire new dress.

Dressed up for courting.

Don't stir the fire with a sword.

Don't make things worse.

His feet are so big he has to put his pants on over his head.

A man with large feet.

You can't tell a man his dog is bad.

People are prejudiced when close friends or relatives are involved.

Let's lay on a lil' more kindlin' wood.

Let's drink some more.

Every dog needs a few fleas.

There is no such thing as a perfect individual.

He'll be late for his own funeral.

A man who is constantly tardy.

Let's call in the dogs and see if they're wet.

I wonder if it's raining outside.

Get your nest built.

Settle down; be still.

The difference between a rat and a squirrel depends on who's doing the eatin'.

Every person has a different outlook.

He keeps right between the bar ditches.

1. He's an honest person. 2. He follows a straight and narrow course.

Don't waste your shells on a dead duck.

Don't worry over matters of inconsequence.

All she has to her name is a Butterick pattern dress.

Poor.

I've been catchin' them faster'n I can string them.

Busy.

There's just as good fish in the creek as ever been caught; there's just as good timber in the woods as ever been bought.

There are still ample opportunities.

I'm ever so much obliged.

Grateful.

You can sow in my field if you want to, but when it comes up, it'll be in yours, and you won't know how it got there.

A rural version of the Biblical admonition, "Whatsoever a man soweth, that shall he also reap."

You can get things fixed, but they won't stay fixed.

Something will eventually go wrong.

He'll make you jump a nine-rail fence.

An influential man.

He moved quicker'n hell can scorch a feather.

Acted hastily.

Hotter'n an oven with the biscuits burning.

Angered.

She's coming across the peach orchard.

A cold northwest wind. In the South, orchards were once planted on the northwest side of the farm.

Welcome as a blowed-down outhouse.

Unwanted.

He was put to bed with a pick and shovel.

Buried.

She's puttin' on airs.

An uppity woman.

That ol' gal was two ax handles wide.

Large, fat.

When you're up to your tail in alligators, you forget that you started out to drain the swamp.

It's hard to keep your objective in mind when you're preoccupied with something else.

You'll find me all right on that, too.

I agree.

You made your bed; now sleep in it.

You caused the problem, you resolve it.

Busier'n a bee in a bottle.

Active.

He had a bilious look.

Sickly.

The East Texas hygiene society.

Buzzards.

I wouldn't trust him any farther than I can throw a bull by the tail.

He isn't very trustworthy.

I covered my back with my belly.

I slept in the open without blankets.

Three bricks short of a load.

He's not too bright.

She thinks she's the greatest thing since sliced bread.

A presumptuous woman.

He can eat corn through a picket fence.

Buck-toothed.

I haven't seen him in a coon's age.

We haven't visited in a long time.

Don't bite off more'n you can chew.

Don't take on too many assignments at one time.

That's mighty high cotton for a country boy.

Plush surroundings.

CHAPTER 5

I hope to be kicked to death by grasshoppers if it ain't the truth.

I'm not lying.

Smells like girls goin' to meeting.

A pleasant odor.

As regular as a goose goes bare-foot.

Consistent in nature.

The only thing he ever ran for was the county line.

A dishonest politician.

Knee-walking, commode-hugging drunk.

Soused.

Keep your forked end down.

Stand on your own two feet; be independent.

Nothing ever went over the back that didn't come back under the belly.

Everything eventually comes full circle.

I've enjoyed as much of this as I can stand.

A miserable experience.

I've got more'n I can say grace over.

Overworked.

I can't gee and haw at the same time.

Unable to do two things at once.

Like driving a herd of hogs.

Disorganized.

Hotter'n blue blazes.

Torrid; a quick temper.

I 'cooned a foot log.

Walked a log across a stream.

He gave her an all-squeezin' hug.

A warm embrace.

He hollered like a stuck hog.

He was deceived.

He has one foot in the grave and the other on a banana peel.

1. Near death. 2. Approaching a serious crisis.

He raised hell and stuck a chunk under it.

A display of anger.

Put the food in the wagon; the hogs are loose.

Exercise some caution.

He pulled his freight in a hurry./He ran like the devil was chasing him.

Moved quickly.

That horse will throw him so high that the birds'll build nests in his ears before he hits the ground.

A wild bucking horse.

Where cobwebs grow, no beau will go.

An untidy house isn't likely to attract a husband.

He won't stay hitched.

Lacks commitment.

Suckin' hind teat.

Lacks full acceptance.

Happy as a dead pig in the sunshine.

Satisfied.

She has legs like a Tennessee walking horse.

Shapely.

He's selling hogs to buy feed.

Poor management.

He's studying to be a half-wit, and I'm afraid he ain't gonna make it.

Lacks wisdom.

My ol' heart was thumping like the devil beating tanbark.

1. Excitable. 2. In love.

Every ol' hen thinks her chick is the best.

Everybody has a certain measure of pride.

He's a hundred dollar saddle and a twenty dollar horse man.

Lacks a sense of value.

He looks like he swallowed all of a white horse 'cept the tail.

A bewhiskered fat man.

Let's fatten a hog.

Let's celebrate.

Head hog at the trough.

A person of importance.

Damn a house with one door.

No avenue of escape.

All wool and a yard wide.

Of considerable substance; a respected individual.

He bellered like a bay steer.

He was upset.

If your pearls ain't polished, they can't shine.

The good things in life require some effort.

You don't allow?

Do you mean it?

Allowing as how...

Considering the circumstances...

You might as well argue with a wooden Indian.

Useless.

Eyes bigger'n saucers.

Surprised; excited.

Six of one and a half-dozen of another.

It's all the same.

He put the hairy eyeball on him.

He examined him closely; suspicious.

He's gritty as fish eggs.

Unafraid.

He's the kind who'll cut a man's trotline.

Untrustworthy.

I took my foot in my hand and walked.

I did it my way.

Even a fish wouldn't get caught if he kept his mouth shut.

Be careful in conversation.

The fat's in the fire.

Trouble.

How's momma and them?

A greeting meaning, "How are you?"

Take a 'tater and wait.

Be patient.

Granny was an all-standing tough ol' gal.

A respected woman.

He don't stand a cut dog's chance.

It isn't likely to happen.

Get your tail out from 'neath your legs.

Stop feeling sorry for yourself.

It's time to wet on the fire and call in the dogs.

Time to go home.

If you sleep with dogs, you'll wake up with fleas.

If you associate with bad company, you can expect a poor reputation.

Tighter than a duck's end.

Stingy.

Deader'n a door knob (or nail).

Lifeless.

Dead and too dumb to fall over.

Ignorant.

Dry as a cow chip.

Thirsty.

Crooked as a dog's hind leg.

Dishonest.

He has diarrhea of the jaw.

Talkative.

A diarrhea of words and a constipation of thoughts.

Meaningless conversation.

That takes the cake.

That's something.

Dirt shows up on the cleanest cotton.

Misdeeds by a pious individual are evident to everyone.

What can't be cured must be endured.

If you can't do something about a problem, learn to live with it.

Let her alone and she'll come home to her milk.

She'll do the proper thing if given a chance.

Come light; go light.

Don't overburden yourself.

Cold as a well-digger's rear.

Frigid weather.

Lick by lick, the cow ate the grind-stone.

Nothing is impossible.

I owe my soul to the company store (or the commissary).

I'm in debt.

I ain't seen a crop yet that'll grow by the light of the moon.

An impossibility.

It takes him forever to 'coon a tree.

Moves slowly.

No deeper than a heavy dew./Not deep enough to float a match./Shallow as a puddle.

Lacking in depth.

Don't that beat all?

Isn't that something?

If you make your bed hard, you can turn over oftener.

The easy way isn't always the best way.

He's trying to throw a wide loop with a short rope.

He's trying to be something he isn't.

He butters his bread on both sides.
Successful.

There's a fly in the buttermilk.
A delicate situation.

He's bellyin' through the brush.
Avoiding the law.

Biggety and overbearing.
Domineering.

Bright-eyed and bushy-tailed.
Enthusiastic.

A bird in the hand causes a big mess.
Things aren't always what they seem to be.

I've got to run home and build a cake.
I've got some baking to do.

She found tracks in the yard.
She suspects her husband of being unfaithful.

Nothing dries as quick as a tear.
All problems soon pass.

Not as big as a minute.
Little.

Keep your mouth wet and your feet dry.

A good way to avoid a cold.

She was madder'n a wet hen.

Angry.

Hoover hogs.

Armadillos.

Goat-roper.

A country boy.

Busier'n a funeral home fan at a July revival.

Active.

Foot-loose, fancy-free.

Unfettered.

I came to town to see the fat lady.

I'm curious about what's happening.

It was a duster.

An unproductive effort. A term first coined by oilmen to indicate a dry hole.

Well, that's another day, another dollar.

The job is finished.

Dinner on the grounds.

A meal served outdoors, usually at a church function.

Jitney.

A small wornout automobile.

I feel like I been drug through hot coals face-first.

Feverish.

Wings don't mean a chicken can fly.

Some things aren't what they appear to be.

CHAPTER 6

He's one of the finest God ever wallowed a chitlin' in.

A person of admirable qualities.

Six ways from Sunday.

Confusion.

Chicken one day, feathers the next.

Prosperity today, poverty tomorrow.

He did me dirt.

He insulted me.

I'll strap a deal on you that Babbo won't take off.

I'll offer you a good trade.

We've howdyed but we ain't shook.

We haven't been formally introduced.

She's meaner'n a biting sow.

Quick to anger.

He's all beer and no foam.

An individual of high esteem. Some East Texans use the expression in reverse, "He's all foam and no beer".

The little bird who chirps in the morning is likely to be hawk bait by nightfall.

A boastful person will come to a tragic end.

I've been sitting in the back singing bass.

I'm minding my own business.

I feel like I've been rode hard and put up wet.

Exhausted.

Her face caught fire and somebody put it out with an ax.

Unattractive.

Uglier than seven miles of bad roads.

Unbecoming.

Let's get shed of that.

To dispose of something.

I'm dragging my dobber in the dirt.

Weary.

You can't do business with an empty wagon.

It is fruitless to deal with a shallow person.

We've been plowing too close to the cotton.

We haven't exercised enough caution.

Catty-wampus.

1. Indirect. 2. Somewhat adjacent to something.

That was a real clear-up shower.

It rained clear up to the front porch.

He kicked my tail 'till my nose started bleeding.

I lost the fight.

If the Good Lord's willing and the creek don't rise.

If nothing happens.

Jug-butted.

A broad-bottomed man.

She's idlesome minded.

Disorganized.

Big talker, little doer.

Braggart.

I had to shake the trees for him.

Conducted a search.

Short visits make long friends.

Don't overstay your welcome.

Weather cold enough to freeze the horns off a brass billy goat.

Frigid weather.

He totes water on both shoulders.

He often takes both sides of an issue.

It was a goose drownder.

A hard rainfall.

She's got a warm corner coming.

An elderly person.

Between hay and grass.

Spring is approaching.

If it thunders before seven, it'll rain before eleven.

Rain is approaching.

Quit your wartin' me.

Stop annoying me.

Preacherfied.

Pious.

She can throw out more with a tea-spoon than a working man can bring in with a shovel.

Unlikely to recognize value.

That was something to write home about.

Good news.

Don't crow until you get out of the woods. The sheriff may be hidin' behind the last tree.

Be cautious.

The worm is the only animal that don't fall down.

Don't be overly concerned if you fail.

It'll have to get worse before it gets better.

The need to resolve an issue may have to be put into sharper focus before a solution can be found.

You can tell him by the rattle of his wagon.

A shallow man.

Keep one eye open for snakes and the other for bees.

Remain alert.

Poor-boying.

Doing something cheaply.

He's butting his brains on a stooping post oak.

Putting an end to a worthless existence.

A feller who gets all wrapped up in hisself makes a pretty little package.

A pompous man has little respect.

Hotter'n a peddler's pistol.

Stolen.

Muddy roads call the mile post a liar.

Bad roads seem longer than they really are.

Road rough as a washboard.

Poor roads.

If that had been a snake, it would've bit you.

It was right under your nose all the time.

He's so tenderhearted he couldn't stand to see his wife work. So he put on his hat and went to town.

Lazy and inconsiderate.

He's taken to eatin' razor soup.

Caustic, quick to criticize.

Sweep before your own door.

Don't criticize others if you're guilty of the same fault.

Independent as a wood sawyer.

Self-sufficient.

Light a shuck.

Do it quickly.

We have a good season in the ground.

The prospects are good for a profitable crop.

He's thumbing the scales.

Cheating.

She's too slow to catch a cold.

Sluggish in nature.

Like trying to scratch your ear with your elbow.

An effort that cannot produce results.

Strong as horseradish.

Influential.

He's walking for a wagon.

Walking quickly.

There's many a slip between the cup and the lip.

A lot of things can happen to change the best-laid plans.

The time to kill a snake is when he raises his head.

1. Be decisive in your actions. 2. When a problem arises, attend to it.

Stick with me and you'll be sneezing through silk.

I'll make you prosperous.

It's time to put the tools in the truck.

Time to go home.

It serves the worm right for getting up so early.

A just reward for an over-anxious effort.

A sun sets red and brings rain on a traveler's head.

A red sunset is likely to precede rain.

Ugly as a wart on a pickle.

Homely.

Frozen stiff as stilliards.

Cold.

A little powder and a little paint will make a woman what she ain't.

Cosmetics will work wonders.

A dry well teaches us the worth of water.

We seldom appreciate the best things in life.

A woman, a dog and a walnut tree; the harder you beat them, the better they be.

Sterness produces results.

A woman, a cat and a chimney should never leave the house.

Each has its own place.

Cut your peaches, girls, thunder ain't rain.

Finish your work, there's still time.

He was treed by his own woman.

He was unfaithful, and his wife found out.

His daddy gave him a woodshed lecture.

His father whipped him.

I only have time for a whore bath.

Using perfume and deodorant.

A whistling woman and a crowing hen never came to a very good end.

Don't pretend to be something you aren't.

Well-whetted, half-cut.

Be prepared before you undertake a job and the task will be easier.

He was hung by the neck 'till honest.

Hanged.

They were caught talking to catfish.

Caught using electrical apparatus to illegally shock fish in the water, a practice often called "telephoning".

That'll damn well fix Oscar.

The job has been completed.

Never mind the mule. Keep loading the wagon.

Don't be distracted.

As much as flies love Flit.

Distasteful.

CHAPTER 7

I was joobus of him.

Suspicious.

Homely as a Montgomery Ward woman sent west on approval.

Unattractive.

Quick stitches save the britches.

Early action produces results.

He broke a trace chain to help out.

He made a sacrifice.

Every chimney smells of smoke sooner or later.

Unwanted but unavoidable.

I'm put out with him.

Annoyed.

He's top water minnow.

Lacking in quality.

I've got bigger fish to fry.

I've got more important things to do.

He has more guts than you can hang on a fence.

Unafraid.

Whistling through the graveyard.

Building up courage or confidence.

He cut out for home like a cane-break fire.

Moved quickly.

There are better ways to kill a dog than by choking him to death on hot butter.

There are more effective ways to achieve results.

Let sleeping dogs lie./Don't go around kicking dogs.

Don't look for trouble.

That was the last button on old Gabe's coat.

The last straw.

Don't dare kiss an ugly girl; she'll tell the whole darn world.

Unattractive women are likely to brag of their romances.

I got a bread 'n butter invitation.

An invitation to dinner.

They limb-skinned and jay-hawked that tree.

Went up a tree in search of a raccoon.

Since hell was a pup.

A long time ago.

She's independent as a hog on ice.

Self-centered.

He bounces around like a hicker-nut in a wagon bed.

1. Lacks direction. 2. Disorganized.

Sharp as a briar.

Intelligent.

He looks like he just stepped out of a band box.

A flashy dresser.

The broom's behind the door.

Prepare for the arrival of visitors.

Don't believe everything you hear, and only half of what you see.

Be skeptical.

Go back on it.

To change your mind.

Don't throw out the baby with the bathwater.

Separate the good from the bad.

Foot-washing Baptist.

A term applied to a little-known Baptist faith.

One good turn gets most of the bed-sheet.

Courtesy pays dividends.

Birds can't fly on one wing.

Don't leave a job half-finished.

She's rushing around like a chicken with its head cut off.

Disorganized.

I can't cotton to that.

I don't like it.

My crop is laid by.

Finished.

It's as dark as the inside of a gunny sack.

Without light.

Sunday go-to-meeting clothes.

Wearing your best suit or dress.

Let's wait 'till we see how the cat jumps.

Be patient.

He did it in two shakes of a cow's tail.

In a hurry.

He let the cat out of the wallet (or box).

He revealed a secret.

Kissing don't last; cooking does.

You can't live on love alone.

Sure as a dog will howl at the moon.

I'm positive.

A bit dog never barks.

A man who suffers one mistake isn't likely to make the same one again.

He brung up the drags.

Tired.

To the lame and the blind, a one-eyed man is king.

1. Everyone has some admirers. 2. There's always a silver lining.

You can't hear your ears in this place.

Noisy.

He's playing a hand with his eyes shut.

Taking a chance.

A wind from the west, and the fish bite best.

A fishing adage.

Let's step and fetch it.

Quickly.

I'd like to put a log on the fire.

I'm interested.

He flung me away.

He threw me down, or away from him.

It's coming grass.

Spring is near.

Clothes-line talk./Back-fence business./Picket-fence patter.

Gossip.

Greedy as a hog.

A glutton.

She's always wantin' to eat in the next pasture.

Looking for better opportunities.

Boys, the hogs are crossing the river.

The water in the river is low.

I'd like to whoa up on that.

Give me a chance to think.

Don't kick 'till you're spurred.

Don't act prematurely.

It'll be a cold day in hell (or a cold day in August).

It will never happen.

That ol' pony paces like a rocking chair.

An easy-riding horse.

Lift up your carcass.

Stand up and be counted.

She's living high on the hog.

Prosperous.

He's a three thousand man.

A productive worker.

Don't shoot your horse 'cause you don't like the way the race was run.

Don't cut off your nose to spite your face.

Nervous as an ol' hog on a cold morning.

Agitated.

If you have enough horse sense to treat your wife like a racehorse, she'll never become a nag.

Treat your wife well and she'll return the favor.

Feed a cold, starve a fever.

Eat and drink a lot to combat a cold.

You can take the boy out of the country, but you can't take the country out of the boy.

You can't change some people.

Your chickens will come home to roost.

Be careful in what you do and say.

Don't get your feathers ruffled.

Don't be upset.

Stretch your gingham, girl.

Pull down your dress.

We go to bed with the chickens (or get up with the chickens).

We retire early (or arise early).

A rich bride goes young to church.

A wealthy woman marries early.

He's been draggin' that cotton sack too long.

Weary from working too long on one project.

Every dog has his day.

Even the most worthless individual has some value.

The man who dances has to pay the fiddler.

You have to pay for what you get.

She's sticking like a sick kitten to a hot brick.

Persistent.

He's a going-Jessie.

Am ambitious person.

High-binder.

Shyster.

Slick as a greased hog.

Elusive.

If you can't listen, maybe you can feel.

A mother's threat to spank her children.

Them that has must lose 'cause them that hasn't can't.

There's a difference between being rich and poor.

You can judge a man by the horse he rides.

A man picks surroundings which reflect his personality.

Get high behind.

Devote more attention to your task.

Shotgun house.

A small house, usually long and narrow.

Fatback.

Fatty pork.

Them hogs scattered everywhichaways.

Dispersed.

That beast has a bellyfull of bedsprings.

A bucking horse.

Honky-tonk.

Saloon or tavern in a rural area.

CHAPTER 8

Let's yank a plank off the wall.

Let's celebrate.

Never leave the mark of the pot on the ashes.

Don't say something you'll later regret.

He promised me a slice of the moon, and gave me a slice of a cow-chip.

Shallow promises.

Touchy as a mule with a tick in his ear.

Sensitive.

Bell the mare.

To get married.

He's struttin' his okra.

Bragging.

Big as a skinned mule and twice as ugly.

A large, unbecoming man.

I saved my manners and my 'possum.

Turned down an invitation to dine.

He put on a whispering campaign.

To spread rumors; usually used in a political campaign.

Every time I stand up, my mind sits down.

Unable to think clearly.

Don't let your mouth overload your tail.

Don't talk too much.

It would draw blisters on a rawhide boot.

Moonshine liquor.

She'll marry at the drop of a hat, and throw it herself.

Looking for a husband.

If I had to marry her, I'd draw straws and marry the straw.

She's not the woman I want to marry.

That ol' horse has been shod all 'round.

Married four times.

She's wishing she was back under momma's bed playing with the kittens.

Longing for home.

She hung the moon.

Respected, beloved.

I'm feeling middling fair.

My health is improving, but it could be better.

Long as a country mile.

A considerable distance.

It's like talking Chinese to a cow.

1. An unproductive effort. 2. It doesn't make sense.

That was a larrapin' good meal.

Delicious.

A miss is good as a mile.

The mistake can't be corrected.

Sawmill license./Cotton-patch license.

Married without a legal ceremony.

I wouldn't marry him if he was the last man on God's green earth.

I don't want him for my husband.

He was all-scarin' mad.

Frightened and angry.

They jumped the broom.

Married.

He put the bad mouth on it.

To insult something.

There's a family difference 'tween the mule and the singletree.

A husband and wife don't always agree.

Out of pocket.

Unavailable. A similar term, used in England, means "out of money".

She got her nose out of joint.

Peeved.

Any ol' mule's tail can catch cockle burrs.

That job isn't so difficult.

Kicking won't get you anywhere unless you're a mule.

Complaining won't help.

My ox is in the ditch.

I'm in trouble.

He gored my ox.

He caused the trouble.

He was caught with his pants down.

Embarassed.

Her pictures are used to wean heifers.

Ugly.

Pretty as a speckled pup under a red wagon.

Cute, adorable.

Grinnin' like a 'possum.

An embarassed smile.

Don't fret.

Don't worry.

His pistol was cocked and primed.

Prepared.

It ain't worth a Continental damn.

Of little value.

He's a regular wheel horse.

Someone of considerable energy.

He'll work from Ken to Kent./He'll work from can to can't.

An energetic worker.

Tumped over.

Overturned.

Dew claw.

A bad toe on a dog's leg.

Teched.

Addled.

He took me to the tall timbers.

He beat me in a contest.

Peckerwood sawmill.

A small sawmill.

We came through by the Smiths.

We took a short cut.

He stobbed me.

He stabbed me with a knife.

He's a stem-winder and a go-getter.

A man who puts out a lot of effort.

Throwin' your rope before you make a loop ain't gonna catch the cow.

Be prepared before you act.

Four sights down the road.
A long distance.

He prized off a window.
He broke into the house by removing a window.

I'll clean your plow.
To punish.

Hold your 'tater until mine gets cold.
Wait for me.

She sure pleasured me.
She did something nice for me.

That ol' woman was raised on prunes and proverbs.
A pious woman.

More'n Carter has pills.
Ample.

High, wide and handsome.
A happy, fat person.

It's a fur piece yonder.
A long distance.

Limber-legged./Skunk drunk.
Inebriated.

Drunk, dressed up and no place to go.

He has no purpose to his life.

He's draggin' his navel in the dirt.

Moving rapidly.

Don't be like the ol' woman who fell out of the wagon.

Don't get so involved you forget what you're doing.

She's galavantin' (or sashayin') all over the county.

Acting uppity.

She's a long-tall Sally.

A tall, good-looking woman.

She sidled up to him.

Flirting.

There's always a best way for doing something.

There's a proper method for everything.

There you go.

I agree.

That's a bunch of bull.

Nonsense.

I'd rather have a tired arm than an empty stomach.

I'd rather work than go hungry.

He's gettin' too big for his britches.

Arrogant.

Let's beat the bushes for him.

Let's search for him.

She has a bee in her bonnet.

She has an idea which bothers me.

Jake-leg carpenter.

A self-taught craftsman.

The canker is in the flower./The weevils are in the flour.

Ruin is likely.

When the cow comes into bucket.

When something happens.

I'll be a bit bugger.

An expression of surprise.

Shack bully.

An overbearing person, usually found around a sawmill.

Paddle your own boat.

Be independent.

He wanted it worse'n I did.

He wanted to buy something I had, so I sold it.

Piddlin' poor.

Not very substantial.

He don't know spit from Shinola.

Bumbling.

CHAPTER 9

Only a fool picks a fight with a mule or a skunk.

Don't be foolish.

The tongue always seeks the tooth that hurts.

The immediate problem gets the most attention.

I don't know him from Adam's ox.

We're not acquainted.

Poor as a sawmill rat.

Poverty-stricken.

He's airing out his lungs.

Cursing.

Don't fish in troubled waters.

Don't cause trouble.

I killed him too dead to skin.

Overkill.

Better to be a nettle in the side of a friend than his echo.

Be honest with your friends; don't deceive them.

He's fishing with rotten string and an empty hook.

Not likely to produce results.

She's hotter'n an old hen in a wool basket.

Angry.

A wink's good as a nod to a blind mule.

1. Whatever you try isn't likely to work. 2. It's all the same.

I was fit to bust a gut.

Hilarious.

High tail it.

Hurry.

Hold your horses.

Wait.

Don't jump the traces.

Don't act without proper planning.

Don't go off half-cocked.

Be prepared.

He's dipped his fingers in the lard jar all his life.

A government employee.

He doesn't have both oars in the water.

Not very intelligent.

She's so ugly she has to sneak up on a mirror.

Homely.

Every man is born free and equal. If he gets married, that's his fault.

Marriage is restrictive.

Flatheads.

Loggers.

A day late, a dollar short.

Overdue.

He has the miseries.

Sickly.

She dropped it like a hot potato.

The subject was forgotten.

I'm picking up the pieces.

I'm correcting my mistakes.

It takes one to know one./Don't call the pot black.

You may be guilty of the same fault.

Let's put the little pot in the big pot.

Let's celebrate.

She sang tribble.

Soprano.

That's stout stuff.

Heady.

Come and sit a spell.

Let's visit.

Slick as a whistle.

Bright.

Where the feathers fly is where the shot lie.

You're on target.

With tobacco juice running out of both sides of his mouth.

A level-headed country boy.

Gussied up like a New Orleans pimp.

Dressed fancy in bright colors.

He has eyes to see and wisdom not to see.

He minds his own business.

Let's whittle this down to size.

Let's make it manageable.

Fat wood./Splinters./Light wood./ Lighter wood./Pine shavings./Kindling.

Small pieces of wood used to start a fire.

Let's talk turkey.

Let's get serious about this business.

Talk is cheap, but it takes money to buy whiskey.

'Let's stop talking and get down to business.

Sawmill director.

A negative businessman.

He was asleep at the switch.

He missed an opportunity.

It's been a greasy year.

The smokehouse is full of meat.

A watched pot never boils.

Be patient.

Stop by and take pot luck.
An invitation to dinner.

I'm in a picklement.
Bothered.

Things have gone to pot.
Deteriorating.

I'm purdy-nigh sure.
I'm almost positive.

He whipped out his baking powder notebook and took down my name.
He wrote my name in a small notebook given to him by a baking powder company.

He's big enough to go to mill.
He's capable of assuming additional responsibility.

A liar needs a good memory.
Lies cause trouble.

Noticeable as a bump on a log.
Doesn't attract much attention.

Do go on.
Don't deceive me.

Yellow janders.
Jaundice.

Easier'n sliding off a greased log backwards.

Effortlessly.

Figures never lie, but liars can figure.

An expression of dishonesty.

Just because a little is good don't mean a lot is better.

Some things are more effective in small doses.

The used key is always shiny.

An active person is the most productive.

A jaybird don't rob his own nest.

Don't taint your own surroundings.

It's a long way from Chloe's house.

A lengthy distance.

Lots of hands make light work, but many mouths make empty dishes.

A job can be done quicker if everybody helps.

He has his head in the halter.

Misled.

Root hog or die.

You're on your own.

He hauled hell out of its shuck.

He caused a lot of trouble.

There ain't no horse that can't be rode; there ain't no man that can't be throwed.

1. Nothing is impossible. 2. No man is perfect.

A faint heart never filled a flush.

Timidity will not produce results.

He's looking for a gnat's bristle.

Critical.

Don't waste your shells on grasshoppers when the crows are eating your corn.

Get your priorities in order.

Loose as a goose./He's like a goose. He wakes up in a new world ever morning.

Disorganized.

She buys crutches for lame ducks.

Spends foolishly.

You can't kill an elephant with a BB gun.

Don't undertake something unless you're sure you can do it.

Don't lay it at my door.

Don't blame me.

Get your ducks in a row.

Get prepared.

As far as the naked eye can see.

A considerable distance.

It looked like a constipated fly.

Spotted in appearance.

She's fractious as a filly.

Tempermental.

It's better to be a young man's fool than an old man's sweetheart.

Enjoy youth while you have it.

What you don't have in your hand, you ought to have in your feet.

If it doesn't work one way, try another.

A fool and his money are soon parted, and a fool and your money are probably running for reelection.

Beware of politicians.

Better'n a brick outhouse.

Something to be admired.

When she says frog, he jumps.

He's henpecked.

He's meeting hisself coming back from where he's been.

Consumed with work.

He went whole hog.

Wholly dedicated to an effort.

Put that in your pipe and smoke it.

Here's something to consider.

If I tell you a hen totes cotton, you can hitch her up.

You can be assured I'm telling you the truth. Another version: "If I tell you a hen dips snuff, you can look under her wing."

CHAPTER 10

He's ugly as a tow-sack shirt.

Unattractive.

Like trying to warm up leftover snow.

Out of the question.

Still as a plate of spit.

Calm, hushed.

She has about as much to offer as a poor pullet.

Unable to contribute greatly.

It was stronger'n a mare's breath.

Potent.

Give me some lick on my dodger.

Put some syrup on my cornbread.

This is like herding guineas.

Disorganized.

I've been to three county fairs, two goat-ropings and a 'tater digging.

I know what's going on; I've been around.

He has book-learning and hog-sense.

He's educated, but lacks common sense.

Stronger than seven acres of garbage.

Tenacious, powerful.

I can explain it to him, but I can't understand it for him.

Thick-headed.

Like carrying a chicken to Sunday School.

Not very practical.

Somebody threw a dead cat down the well.

Someone is causing trouble.

We used her biscuits to chunk the dogs.

A poor cook.

He's boot-broke and hat-happy.

A drugstore cowboy.

He has a brittle backbone.
Cowardly.

He has an alligator mouth and a hummingbird behind.
A small person with a loud mouth.

Chunk-floater (mover)./Frog-strangler./Dam-buster./Stump-mover./ Trash-floater.
A hard rain.

He's hiding behind his momma's apron.
Cowardly.

He's just a clabber-headed ol' boy.
Slow-witted.

He couldn't run a watermelon stand if you gave him the watermelons and the Highway Patrol flagged the traffic.
Lack of administrative ability.

It's hog-killin' weather.
Cold.

Big as a No. 3 washtub.
Large.

Look out for skinny bankers and fat congressmen.

Exercise caution.

He ain't got no more sense than God gave a goose.

Ignorant.

His get-up and go has got up and went.

He lost his enthusiasm and energy.

He couldn't drive a wheelbarrow.

Inept.

Like trying to fetch water in a peach basket.

Not very practical.

It was tasty as lard.

Unappetizing.

Who set your tail feathers a-fire?

Who made you mad?

He's got no more sense than a little boy with a big navel.

Slow-witted.

Spit and whittlers./Hangers-on.

Loafers. Usually found around a country store.

He's like a bull in a china closet.

Has little tact.

He broke out with a case of the runs.

Frightened.

They're like two peas in a pod.

Constant companions.

She stuck to him like hot pine rozzum.

Stayed close.

It's still as a pig a-wettin'.

1. Quiet. 2. Inactive.

There's yellowjackets in the outhouse.

Trouble.

He'd brag about the number of holes in his outhouse.

Boastful about everything.

She wove at him.

Waved a greeting.

He's a hatchet man.

Someone who carries out distasteful assignments for another person.

Like whupping a dead horse.
Pursuing a lost cause.

She wears her feelings on her sleeve.
Offends easily.

He has a face like an open field.
Unable to hide emotions.

She's touchy as a fat fryer on Sunday.
Sensitive.

Friendly as fire ants.
Hostile.

He couldn't count to 20 with his shoes off.
Not too smart.

My tail's a-dragging./My bottom's a-dragging./I'm dragging bottom.
Tired.

He's holdin' a dead man's hand.
His luck is running out.

Ol' biddy.
A troublesome woman.

I've got dirt to scratch and eggs to lay.

I've got things to do.

Yaller dog Democrat./Brass collar Democrat.

A steadfast member of the Democratic Party.

You can keep a dog, but you only feed a cat.

Dogs respond to affection; cats do not.

The more straws you got in a broom, the more dust you can sweep.

There's strength in numbers.

Cute as a bug's ear.

Adorable.

You can cut off a dog's tail, but you can't sew it back.

1. A bad mistake can't be corrected. 2. Make sure of your intent and purpose before you start something.

I don't care what you call me as long as you call me to supper.

I love to eat.

He's tearing up the patch.

Aggressive, hard-working.

We're farming on thirds and fourths.

Sharecropping.

He hasn't seen his feet in forty years.

A fat man.

There's no fool like an old fool.

Foolishness is seldom tolerated among the elderly.

He'd foul up a two-car funeral.

Error-prone.

He acts like he has fire ants up his leg.

Upset.

You're better'n an acre of pregnant red hogs.

Valuable.

He's slippier'n a boiled onion.

Elusive.

Her backside shakes like a pair of wild hogs in a tow sack.

A fat woman.

She has the green apple nasties.

She is irritable.

Great gobs of galloping goose grease.

An expression of surprise.

They're too poor to paint and too proud to whitewash.

Poor but proud.

It rained hub deep to a ferris wheel.

A hard rain.

It would make a glass eye cry.

Sad.

His teeth are like stars; they come out at night.

Wears falseteeth.

She's five pounds in a three-pound sack.

Fat.

He was so angry he was spitting a stream the size of a handsaw.

Very upset at something.

Hotter'n a burning stump.

Mad and upset.

He cut a fat hog.

He made a notable achievement.

What in a cornbread hell is going on?

What do you mean?

Politicians are like cockroaches. It's not what they carry off, but what they fall into and mess up.

Graft isn't the real problem with politics; it's inefficiency.

Plain as a goat's rear headed uphill.

Obvious.

That fellow would drown a widow woman's ducks.

Mean and devious.

If you put his brains in a bumblebee, he would fly backwards.

Not very bright.

He's lighter than a June frost.

Don't count on him when the chips are down.

Smells worse'n an acre of garlic.

Odorous.

Busier than worms on a bed of hot coals.

Active.

INDEX

111

113

114

117

118

120

121

DATE